AF399897

YOUTUBE: THE HOME OF VLOGGING

The rise of video on demand

Written by Charlotte Bouillot
Translated by Emma Hanna

Business 50MINUTES.com

YOUTUBE: THE HOME OF VLOGGING

Whether they want to express a political opinion, learn how to fix their stove, watch a film clip or a music video by an artist from anywhere in the world, or find out more about the lifestyle of the inhabitants of an island on the other side of the globe, YouTube attracts an audience of a billion internet users who watch a total of six billion hours of video content hosted on the site each month – and all for free!

What was originally envisioned as a simple video-sharing platform now accounts for nearly 4% of internet traffic worldwide. As such, there are some who do not hesitate to say that YouTube has changed the world by making it smaller and more universally accessible. It has opened new doors to fame and fortune, it has given a wide range of political causes and initiatives a voice, and it has revolutionised the way we think about entertainment and education.

Naturally, having dramatically altered the global audiovisual media landscape, YouTube came with the same slew of legal, financial and technical problems common to any new way of doing things. The website was purchased by the American internet giant Google less than two years after it was launched, and evolved in tandem with both the older corporation and the habits of the users who keep it alive. In 2015, YouTube celebrated its 10-year anniversary, and since then has increasingly been turning its attention towards cementing its position as the leader of the ultra-competitive but tremendously profitable sector of on-demand video, despite being faced with powerful competitors with near-bottomless funds to draw on.

KEY INFORMATION

- **Founders:** Chad Hurley (American entrepreneur, born in 1977), Steve Chen (Taiwanese-American entrepreneur, born in 1978) and Jawed Karim (German-American IT specialist and entrepreneur, born in 1979).
- **Founded:** the domain name youtube.com

was registered on 14 February 2005.
- **Commercial launch:** a beta version of the site was launched in May 2005, and it officially went public in November of the same year.
- **Sector:** online video hosting.
- **Key figures:**
  - June 2006: almost 20 million unique monthly visitors.
  - October 2007: 100 million videos watched per day worldwide.
  - October 2009: one billion videos watched per day.
  - May 2010: two billion videos watched per day by an average of 500 million monthly visitors.
  - October 2010: one billion subscribers to YouTube's user-created "channels".
  - May 2011: more than three billion videos watched per day; 48 hours' worth of video content uploaded to the site per minute.
  - May 2012: over 72 hours' worth of video content watched on the site per minute; 4 billion videos watched per day worldwide by 800 million users (of

whom 136 million originated from the United States).

- ° May 2013: one billion users; more than 100 hours' worth of video content uploaded to the site per minute.
- ° November 2014: over 300 hours' worth of video content uploaded to the site per minute.
- ° February 2017: over 400 hours' worth of video content uploaded to the site per minute; one billion hours' worth of video content watched per day.

- **Key terms:**
  - ° **Blog:** a website where an internet user regularly publishes personal reflections or articles about a specific topic. The word was originally a portmanteau of the words "web" and "log", and blogs have sometimes been likened to online journals. They are characterised by tremendous freedom of expression compared to institutional media outlets which follow a very particular editorial line, and by frequent interaction with readers through the use of hyperlinks, comments and links to social media.

- **Vlog:** this newer form of blogging uses videos as a medium, often in combination with captions or images, to approach all kinds of topics in an informal way. Today, YouTube is the most influential vlogging platform, and hosts the videos uploaded by the record-holder for the highest number of consecutive daily posts on a personal vlog: Charles Trippy, an American vlogger who has posted 3057 consecutive daily vlogs on YouTube as of 14 September 2017 (Guinness World Records, 2017).
- **Copyright:** a form of intellectual property law which grants the creator of a literary, artistic or scientific work, or the creator's representative, the exclusive right to use and reproduce that work.

CONTEXT

FROM BLOGGING...

As recently as the early 2000s, creating websites and sharing content online was the sole domain of the IT elite with their expert knowledge of HTML, but this is almost unimaginable today.

HTML

The computing language HTML (HyperText Mark-Up Language) is one of the three key inventions which became the cornerstones of the internet in its earliest form, along with the HTTP protocol and web addresses. This standard language was developed in the early 1990s and allows the creator of a web document to include formatting and links to other web content while writing it.

Blogger.com was launched in August 1999 as a way to give ordinary people a voice on the internet. Most of the services offered by the platform are free of charge, making it extremely simple to publish content on the internet. Although it got off to a shaky start, the website went on to attract over a million users and was purchased by Google four years after it was created. This was a strategic acquisition for the web giant: at that point, blogging was steadily becoming more popular and seemed likely to trigger great changes in the way information was spread online. At a time when mainstream media was controlled by multinational corporations, the blog emerged as an indispensable means of communication for smaller associations and began springing up throughout the political sphere, in universities, and in the world of business. David Krane, who was the director of corporate communications at Google at the time, described it as "a global self-publishing phenomenon that connects Internet users with dynamic, diverse points of view while also enabling comment and participation" (Gillmor 2003).

...TO VLOGGING

YouTube was not the first online video hosting service to appear (for example, ShareYourWorld. com was launched in 1997), but it was the first site to opt for a novel means of operating. Previously, users had to download a file in order to view it, but streaming technology now makes it possible to view a video while it is being broadcast online. Furthermore, the site is free to use, unlike most other content hosting platforms which were available at that time, which generally operated on a system of paid subscriptions. Users can access the site's videos directly by using a web browser, without having to install and figure out how to use specific programmes for uploading or downloading content (images, music, videos, etc.) or to code, compress and format the files. Quite the contrary: once the files have been uploaded to the internet, sharing them on your own website or on social networks is child's play. From June 2005 onwards – only four months after the website was launched – it was already possible to embed a YouTube video player on any webpage.

Although many sites which were active at that time enabled users to share photos free of charge, most of them were primarily oriented towards selling personalised gifts or digital photo printing services. Meanwhile, although online video sharing had opened up a world of endless possibilities for internet users, the sector had not yet found a suitable economic model. Jakob Lodwick, one of the founders of Vimeo, the American community-based website founded in November 2004, admitted: "We put up the site to see what would happen" (Graham 2005).

In July 2006, a YouTube video hit one million views for the first time. The video in question was an advert for the American sportswear brand Nike featuring the Brazilian footballer Ronaldinho which had gone viral. In fact, the brand was one of the first companies to sense the platform's potential as a promotional vehicle. According to the New York-based data analysis service Hitwise, Inc., by the end of September 2006 almost half of American internet users looking for online videos used YouTube. In August 2007, the platform began monetising this traffic by integrating advertising into the videos it hosts.

THE EARLY DAYS

THE FOUNDERS

Jawed Karim was the first person to post a video on YouTube. The video in question, titled "Me at the zoo", was posted on 23 April 2005, and shows the young IT specialist at San Diego zoo talking about the size of the elephants' trunks for 18 seconds. The video has now reached over 42 million views.

This young graduate from the University of Illinois at Urbana-Champaign was part of a trio who met while working for PayPal – the online payment service founded in 1998 and purchased by eBay in 2002 – and who went on to found YouTube in 2005. Karim was born in Germany in 1979 to a Bengali father and a German mother. He and his entire family immigrated to the United States when he started high school.

Along with Steve Chen, an American entrepreneur of Taiwanese descent and a fellow Illinois graduate, Karim took charge of the technical aspects of the site's development. After his stint at PayPal, Chen worked for Facebook, the American social network founded in 2004, for a few months before leaving to co-found YouTube and lead the company's technical department. However, Karim eventually opted to take on the role of an external consultant while he continued with his studies.

Meanwhile, the third founder, Chad Hurley, was the one who registered the brand, logo and domain name of youtube.com on 14 February 2005, and who served as the company's CEO until October 2010. This sporty, artistic young American entrepreneur holds a joint degree in Information Technology and Fine Art from Indiana University of Pennsylvania. Having finished his studies, he heard about the imminent launch of PayPal and offered his services as a graphic designer to create a logo for the company. Along with Chen and Karim, he became one of the company's first employees, before leaving it together a few years later, having scraped together the necessary funds to found YouTube.

The first version of YouTube that was created by its three founders was a dating site called Tune In Hook Up, which allowed its users to rate the attractiveness of the ads published online. However, this site only lasted for a few weeks. The first seeds that led to the creation of YouTube as we know it today were planted in 2004, when Karim had difficulty finding content online, specifically images showing the tsunami that struck Indonesia that year and a recording of Janet Jackson's wardrobe malfunction at the Super Bowl. Hurley and Chen also had difficulties when they tried to share a video shot during a dinner in San Francisco.

In November 2005, the California-based venture capital firm Sequoia Capital, which had already provided funding for Cisco Systems, Oracle, Apple and Google, invested $3.5 million in the platform, which made it possible for YouTube to increase its bandwidth, improve its server performance and launch a public version of the site.

The first version of the site's homepage

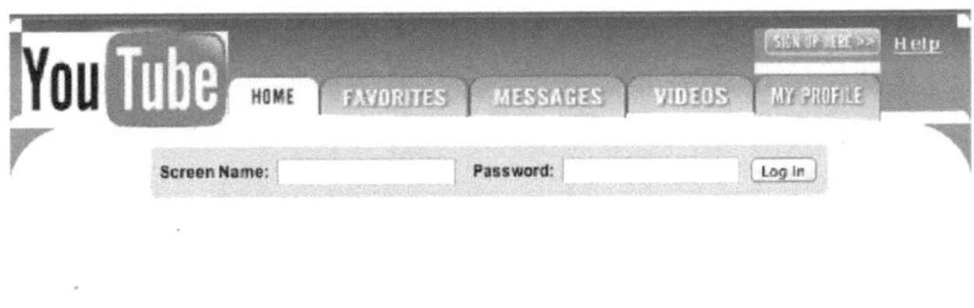

In 2011, Hurley and Chen founded another star-tup together: AVOS Systems, which they later used to launch the video-sharing mobile app MixBit in 2013. At the time they gave a statement saying: "We think video should be a living, breathing entity and that creativity is a collaborative process" (Moscaritolo, 2013).

BROADCAST YOURSELF

Infinite content, accessible to all

As its name and former slogan "Broadcast Yourself" suggest, YouTube's aim is to give individuals the chance to create and share their own videos. In an interview with the Indiana

University of Pennsylvania's magazine, Hurley explained:

> "None of us had any experience with it, but we could see there was a need to be able to share clips from cell phones and other places. If you were viewing on line, half the time, it wouldn't work. We decided to see if we couldn't simplify the whole thing with Flash video." (Gresh 2007)

YouTube is based on very simple operating principles: uploading videos to the site, watching videos that other users have uploaded, and interacting with the videos and with other users by posting comments and video responses. It is not even necessary to create an account or download a particular programme in order to watch videos if you do not want to actively participate in the platform's community. It is as simple as turning the TV on, but with more content, sourced from all over the world, on all kinds of topics, which is available for free and on demand. It is not exactly surprising that the site quickly proved a success!

The ultimate reality TV

By giving users from all over the world the chance to post their personal videos online,

YouTube provided them with a means of unlimited communication, which they could use for any purpose, from rambling about their daily life to showing off their talents or speaking out in favour of a cause. According to IDC, an American market research, analysis and consulting firm, the increasing use of small digital cameras led to a tremendous increase in the volume of video filmed over the course of a single year – from 24 million gigabytes in 2004 to 34 million in 2005. Uploading one of these videos to YouTube is as simple as creating a user account and giving the video a title and short description.

> "People have a lot of different experiences out there, and they want to share them. That's what we're about. We're the ultimate reality TV, giving you a glimpse into other people's lives." (Chad Hurley, quoted in Graham 2005)

Hours' worth of video uploaded per minute (2008-2014)

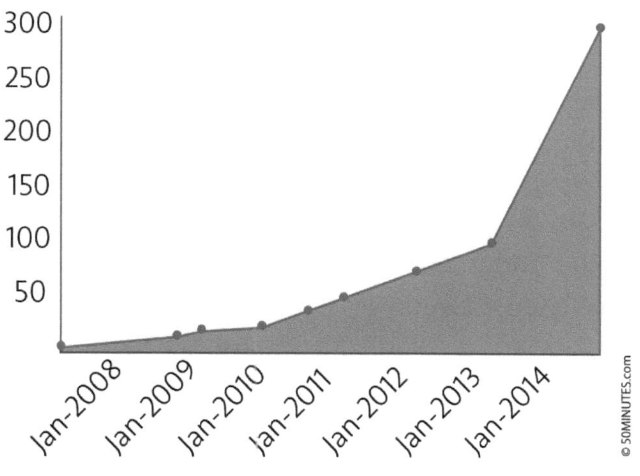

| Source: Youtube.com

Many modern stars launched their careers via YouTube, notably the Canadian singer, actor, dancer and model Justin Bieber, who rose to international fame a few months after posting videos of his performance at his first talent show on YouTube so that his relatives who were unable to attend could watch them. At the time he was only 12 years old and was teaching himself how to play the piano, the trumpet and the guitar. The American agent Scooter Braun stumbled upon some videos in which he played covers of songs by Chris Brown and Usher, and managed to get in contact with the future star. Initially, he published more online content in the form of more videos filmed with a low-resolution camera, which appeared to show Bieber alone at home, in order to keep his fans convinced that he was just like them. He then introduced him to the American R&B singer Usher, who took Bieber under his wing. Today, some of his videos have been viewed over a billion times, and he has performed at Madison Square Garden, at the New Year's countdown hosted by Dick Clark in Las Vegas, and for the American President and First Lady in Washington! According to *Forbes*, he earned over $80 million in 2016.

DID YOU KNOW?

The music video for *Gangnam Style* by the South Korean singer Psy held the title of most-viewed video on YouTube for over four years, but its record was finally broken by the music video for *See You Again* by Wiz Khalifa on 10 July 2017. However, it was less than a month before the top spot was snatched by a different video entirely – on

August 4 2017, the music video for Luis Fonsi's single *Despacito* overtook it, and became the first video on the site to hit 3 billion views on the same day. As of October 2017, the music video for *Despacito*, which was uploaded on 12 January 2017, has over 4 billion views.

YOUTUBE'S EVOLUTION

THE GOOGLE PURCHASE

The start of a revolution

On 9 October 2006 – two years after the site was launched – Google purchased YouTube for the modest sum of $1.65 billion. At that time, 100 million videos, most of which had been created by the users themselves, were uploaded to the site daily. Although it was still a small company with 60 employees at its headquarters in California, YouTube had become the global leader in its sector, holding around 46% of the market share in online video – four times more than the Google Video Store, which was launched in January 2006. Speaking about the purchase, Eric Schmidt, who was the CEO of Google at the time, declared: "This is just the beginning of an Internet video revolution" (cited in La Monica 2006).

Google takes the lead

For Google, this acquisition was a chance to take a shortcut to the forefront of the highly lucrative, fast-growing market of online video, in which many of the key players are social networks. Although most of the billions of video clips streamed each year by the American internet service provider Yahoo had previously been produced professionally, in September 2006 the group announced that it had acquired JumpCut, an online video editor which gave internet users the chance to create their own content. At this point, rumours that the web portal was planning to acquire Facebook were also widespread.

At that time, the world's most popular blogging platform was the Microsoft-owned MSN Spaces, but MSN Video barely managed to reach a market share of over 5%. At the end of 2006, the online video sharing service Soapbox was launched on MSN Video to compete with YouTube; however, its terms of use were much stricter, as it was forbidden to post copyrighted content, and any breaches of this rule led to the video in question being taken down automatically.

CONQUERING THE WORLD

A window to the world

By creating a universally accessible content sharing tool, YouTube's three founders made communication between internet users around the globe practically instantaneous. With just a few clicks of the mouse, it is now possible to find out all about the lives of the people of Iceland, as explained by Icelanders themselves, for example.

Local versions of the site were developed for each country in order to encourage interaction between the site's users. From 2007 onwards, the site began a targeted effort to increase its presence in Europe, using France as a strategic base due to the fact that one of YouTube's main competitors, Dailymotion, is based in France. Dailymotion was launched in March 2005 by the French entrepreneurs Benjamin Bejbaum and Oliver Poitrey, making it the world's very first site where videos could be hosted, shared and viewed for free. In France, both sites attract similar levels of user traffic and have grown at an almost identical rate, which is why YouTube was so keen to launch a French-language version of the site.

Localised versions of the site were also developed in the United Kingdom, Brazil, Ireland, Spain, Italy, Japan, Poland and the Netherlands that year, although in 2008, an option was added that allowed users to change the interface language independently of the version of the site they were accessing.

Diversification of the site's content and audience

- January 2008: a mobile version of the site was launched. By 2015, 50% of the site's traffic was generated by mobile users.
- December 2008: the site – originally a haven for home videos filmed by amateurs – added a setting which made it possible to upload videos in high definition (HD). By 2015, 10% of the videos on the site were available in HD.
- January 2009: the United States Congress created an official YouTube channel; one month later, the Vatican followed suit.
- January 2010: YouTube launched its Video On Demand (VOD) service, following in the footsteps of Netflix (founded in 1997), which

provides an on-demand video subscription service, and Apple, which had been a key figure in the VOD market since 2005 through its iTunes Video Store. YouTube made films by companies such as Disney, Paramount, Sony, Warner Bros. and NBC/Universal available to rent through the site.

- January 2011: more than 400 tweets including a YouTube link were posted per minute, while 150 years' worth of YouTube videos was watched via Facebook per day.
- April 2011: YouTube Live, a feature which made it possible to watch live events, was launched. Events covered by this service included concerts, the Olympic Games, and some of the most highly anticipated current events, such as the British royal wedding of 2011 when Prince William married Kate Middleton, an event which attracted an audience of 72 million on the streaming platform.

VALUE DISTRIBUTION

An unconventional distribution pattern

Although the site was originally envisioned as a way for internet users to share amateur video content, television channels and record labels soon began to view the site as a platform for mass multi-channel distribution, which could be used to create future viral trends. The American broadcasting company NBC, which in February 2006 had demanded that YouTube take down a clip called "Lazy Sunday" from the show Saturday Night Live which had been posted to the site, eventually came to an agreement with YouTube four months later - a partnership which ushered the company into a new digital era. The initial dispute had already pushed YouTube into the spotlight, and the final deal was only the first of many agreements which it eventually signed with major media groups.

In March 2007, the American media giant Viacom, whose subsidiaries include MTV and Paramount Pictures, filed a legal claim against YouTube for massive intentional copyright infringement via 160 000 videos which had amassed a collective view count of over 1.5 billion.

"YouTube has harnessed technology to wilfully infringe copyrights on a huge scale, depriving writers, composers and performers of the rewards they are owed for effort and innovation, reducing the incentives of America's creative industries, and profiting from the illegal conduct of others as well. Using the leverage of the Internet, YouTube appropriates the value of creative content on a massive scale for YouTube's benefit without payment or license." (Viacom 2007)

Content verification

In October 2007, YouTube launched a content verification programme which allows any user to search for videos that they believe to be in breach of copyright and to request their removal. Copyright holders can contribute to a database of information on protected content, which is compared to the videos uploaded to the site. When a match is found, the copyright holders can choose to have the video's audio removed, have it blocked, monetise the video through advertising and/or access statistics regarding the video's user traffic.

Profit distribution

Several other media groups followed in NBC's footsteps to form partnerships with YouTube, notably the American television network CBS and the record labels Sony BMG Entertainment and Universal Music Group. Furthermore, a large number of channels make use of YouTube's Partner Programme.

Producers who demand that the site remove copyrighted content actually end up limiting their audience and create stumbling blocks for their own fans, who generally do not attempt to pirate the content or profit off it by using it illegally. On the other hand, by joining forces with the website, media groups become a part of the shift towards a digital era and are able to make a profit from any content of theirs that is put online. Meanwhile, YouTube cannot make any money from the videos uploaded there without permission from the copyright holders. As such, every video that is verified by Content ID is a new way for YouTube to generate profits, with the copyright holders taking a 90% cut if they decide to monetise the video rather than have it blocked.

This makes YouTube an exceedingly useful tool for professionals who are looking for new ways of managing communication. The video game company Electronic Arts even encouraged internet users to upload videos of their own creatures created using its new game "Spore". Over 100 000 videos were uploaded to the site, which allowed the company to claim a significant profit through the Partner Programme, all while generating a great deal of promotional buzz for the game's release.

In May 2007, YouTube opened the Partner Programme to individuals who posted original content on the platform and had a large follower base. This meant that millions of internet users' pastime of filming themselves in their bedroom with a webcam suddenly became a legitimate way of earning a living. In less than two years, Michael Buckley, the host of a comedy show he had created for YouTube, was making more money from his YouTube videos than from his job as an administrative assistant for the events promotor Live Nation, at which point he resigned in order to devote himself to his show What the Buck? on a full-time basis. At the time, each episode of the show was attracting between 200 000 and 1 million viewers, and he soon earned $100 000 in ad revenue.

YOUTUBE TODAY

A CHANGING ECONOMIC MODEL

Entering the lucrative streaming market

Nowadays, streaming is the name of the game. The key lies in providing a wide range of content which includes both music and video. After several years of being dominated by Spotify, the music streaming market has recently been shaken up, as the internet giants have swept onto the scene.

Although Apple's empire is built on music downloads via iTunes, the company is gradually changing direction. Having purchased Beats by Dr Dre for $2 billion in 2014, Apple now sells the company's famous high-end headphones under its own umbrella and has integrated its streaming service, Beats Music, with its own service, which was rebranded and relaunched on 30 June 2015. Apple Music currently boasts 30 million users worldwide, making it Spotify's main competitor.

In 2014, the American online shopping giant Amazon added a streaming service to the features offered by its premium service, Amazon Prime, for subscribers in the United States, the United Kingdom and Germany. This streaming service offered access to free e-books, films and TV series, as well as over 1 million songs. Amazon's goal is clearly not to revolutionise the market, but to attract even more users to the site so that its overall sales increase.

This trend towards subscription-based services gives YouTube a significant head start on its competitors. In 2015, the platform was attracting over one billion unique visitors per month, 60% of whom used the site to listen to music, a percentage which rose to 90% among 12-24-year-olds, according to a study carried out by Edison Research, solidifying YouTube's position as one of the major online music players. In fact, nine of the platform's ten most-viewed videos are music videos.

Towards paid subscriptions

In 2014, Google announced its plans to launch a music streaming service, which would also provide video streaming. The site's plan was to create a service based on the freemium model (a two-pronged model which includes a free service financed by advertising and a paid, ad-free subscription service), which would see YouTube's music videos separated from the rest of the site's content. The end result, the premium YouTube Red service, features both music and video content and was launched in the United States at the end of October 2015, before being rolled out to four other countries (Mexico, Australia, New Zealand and South Korea) in 2016. The service costs $9.99 per month and allows users ad-free access to all content hosted on the platform, as well as giving them the option to download videos or music to their own devices so that they can be played offline or in the background via the YouTube Music app, and providing access to exclusive series. 55% of the profits from subscriptions are paid directly to creators.

FREEMIUM

The term "freemium" was coined in 2006 by the American researcher and blogger Fred Wilson. It is a portmanteau of the words "free" and "premium", and denotes a business model which consists of two services: one of which is available free of charge, and one of which charges a fee and has improved features. The free service is usually financed by advertising and enables the business to attract a wide range of users who may eventually be persuaded to subscribe to the paid service.

WHAT DOES THE FUTURE HOLD?

The golden age of video on demand

Although YouTube Red is setting itself up as an eventual rival to Netflix, the American company which dominates the market for video on demand thanks to the enormous catalogue of original content available to its subscribers, so far it has mostly been concentrating on a small number of films and series produced by and starring the most popular "youtubers". The first original content released on YouTube Red was *Lazer Team*, a science fiction comedy film produced by Rooster Teeth, an American production company which originated with the creation of a video game-based web series, *Red vs. Blue*, in 2003. Although its content was originally exclusively available through the company's own website, Rooster Teeth eventually became a YouTube partner in 2014. *Lazer Team* was released on January 27 2016, and was followed two weeks later by the premier of *Scare PewDiePie*, a series in which popular Swedish youtuber Felix Kjellberg (better known by his screenname PewDiePie) visits sets based on the horror video games that his 57 million subscribers watch him play and comment on in videos posted to his channel, which is currently the most subscribed on YouTube. As of October 2017, YouTube Red has released just over 20 original series plus 17 original films, the majority of which are comedies and documentaries. By contrast, Netflix – which began producing original content in 2013 – released an estimated 126 original series or films in 2016 alone.

However, there are some who question whether or not YouTube Red's exclusive content is truly worth paying for. The journalist Richard Lawson pulled no punches in his article "Did YouTube Just Ruin YouTube?" which was published in *Vanity Fair* in October 2015, stating "YouTube videos are, by and large, hot stinky garbage. But we watch them, because they are free garbage. And we love free things!" (Lawson 2015).

By late 2016, YouTube Red reportedly had 1.5 million subscribers; however, executives have since declined to reveal more up-to-date figures. It seems clear that the site's greatest challenge in the coming months and years will be to convince its users to pay for a higher-quality service, despite the site's prior lack of fees being one of its main attractions. It therefore comes as no surprise that the *Wall Street Journal* reported that YouTube has made overtures towards Hollywood studios and major production companies regarding potential partnerships. According to a study carried out in 64 countries by the American consulting firm Digital TV Research, the stakes are sky-high for the platform, as the total revenue for the online video streaming sector was estimated at $26 billion for 2015, and is expected to grow to over $51 billion by 2020. Given this context, it is only logical that the internet's largest video sharing network is aiming to claim a sizeable slice of the pie.

DID YOU KNOW?

In the United States, YouTube attracts more viewers aged 18-49 than any television channel.

Related products

According to WebRankInfo, in 2015 over 1 million YouTube channels worldwide generated a profit thanks to the site's Partner Programme. These vlogs, which in many cases have now become veritable brands in their own right, have discovered that any medium can be used to spread their popularity and increase their profits – even good old pen and paper! In 2014, at least a dozen books penned by youtubers hit the bestseller lists, and the numbers have only shot up since then. In an interview with *Mashable* in November 2015, Jeremie Ruby-Strauss, a senior editor for the Gallery Books imprint of the New York publisher Simon and Schuster, explained: "Generally, book publishing is by nature slow to try new things until it sees proof of concept, at which point follows a stampede of acquisition—[which is] often too late" (Hamedy and Franklin 2015).

However, vloggers have an unprecedented advantage: their concept has already been tried, tested and proven by their thousands or even millions of loyal fans. As a result, in 2015, books published by YouTube stars Miranda Sings, Tyler Oakley, PewDiePie and Dan & Phil all hit the *New York Times* bestseller lists, marking the rise of a new genre in the publishing industry.

SUMMARY

- YouTube is an online video sharing platform which was created in 2005 by three former employees of PayPal. Today, an average of one billion hours of content are watched on the site each day, and it accounts for 4% of the webpages accessed by internet users worldwide.
- The site was created with the aim of giving all internet users the opportunity to create, view and share videos for free without having to master HTML coding or download a specific programme. It is as simple as turning the TV on, but with content from all around the world, on all kinds of topics, which is available for free and on demand.
- YouTube is also a powerful way for professionals to communicate with a wider audience, and has fast-tracked several amateur video creators to stardom. One notable example of a celebrity who made their name on YouTube is the Canadian pop star Justin Bieber.
- Less than two years after it was launched, the

site was purchased by Google for the modest sum of $1.65 billion.

- After being accused of illegally profiting from content licenced under copyright, YouTube began using the Content ID detection programme in 2007, which opened the doors to several partnerships with copyright holders so that both sides could profit from ad revenue. The Partner Programme was opened up to amateur content creators soon afterwards. Although the site is tight-lipped about the profits earned by its various partners, it has been revealed that these partners received a combined total of over $1 billion from YouTube between 2007 and 2014.

- 60% of the site's visitors use YouTube to listen to music, which has given the site a head start in the lucrative music streaming market. At the end of 2015, the site launched YouTube Red, a paid subscription service offering ad-free video on demand and unlimited music, proving the site's interest in consolidating a viable economic model.

- Although the total revenue of the online video market was estimated at $26 billion for 2015, and is expected to grow to over $51 billion by

2020, YouTube will have to convince its users to subscribe to a paid service in order to retain its position as the internet's most important online video sharing platform.

We want to hear from you!
Leave a comment on your online library
and share your favourite books on social media!

FURTHER READING

BIBLIOGRAPHY

- Bausch, S. and Han, L. (2006) Youtube U.S. Web Traffic Grows 75 Percent Week Over Week, According To Nielsen//Netratings. *Nielsen Online*. [Online]. [Accessed 11 October 2017]. Available from: <http://www.nielsen-online.com/pr/pr_060721_2.pdf>

- Berg, M. (2015) The World's Highest-Paid YouTube Stars 2015. *Forbes*. [Online]. [Accessed 11 October 2017]. Available from: <http://www.forbes.com/sites/maddieberg/2015/10/14/the-worlds-highest-paid-youtube-stars-2015/>

- Bonanos, P. (2014) Happy Ninth Birthday YouTube: From 'Me at the Zoo' to a Billion Monthly Visits. *Billboard*. [Online]. [Accessed 11 October 2017]. Available from: <http://www.billboard.com/articles/news/6062921/happy-ninth-birthday-youtube-from-me-at-the-zoo-to-a-billion-monthly-visits>

- Courtin, S. (2012) 7 chiffres clés pour les 7 ans de YouTube. *Gentside*. [Online]. [Accessed 11 October 2017]. Available from: <http://www.gentside.com/youtube/7-chiffres-cles-pour-les-7-ans-de-youtube_art40721.html>

- Cuny, D. (2015) YouTube Music, Apple Music, Qobuz : comprendre la jungle du streaming. *L'Obs*. [Online]. [Accessed 11 October 2017]. Available from: <http://rue89.nouvelobs.com/2015/11/25/youtube-music-apple-music-qobuz-comprendre-jungle-streaming-262081>

- Drehs, W. (2015) How PewDiePie gamed the world. *ESPN Magazine*. [Online]. [Accessed 11 October 2017]. Available from: <http://espn.go.com/espn/story/_/id/13013936/pewdiepie-how-became-king-youtube>

- Duffez, O. (2012) YouTube : plein de chiffres et de stats incroyables (août 2017). *WebRankInfo*. [Online]. [Accessed 11 October 2017]. Available from: <http://www.webrankinfo.com/dossiers/youtube/chiffres-statistiques>

- Dumout, E. (2006) CES 2006 – Vidéo à la demande et pack logiciel en téléchargement chez Google. *ZDnet*. [Online]. [Accessed 11 October 2017]. Available from: <http://www.zdnet.fr/actualites/ces-2006-video-a-la-demande-et-pack-logiciel-en-telechargement-chez-google-39301598.htm>

- Fredouelle, A. (2013) Benjamin Bejbaum : jeune provocateur, ex-CEO de Dailymotion. *Le Journal du Net*. [Online]. [Accessed 11 October 2017]. Available from: <http://www.journaldunet.com/ebusiness/le-net/benjamin-bejbaum-benjamin-bejbaum-biographie.shtml>

- Fried, I. (2009) Microsoft gives up YouTube chase.

CNet. [Online]. [Accessed 11 October 2017]. Available from: <http://www.cnet.com/news/microsoft-gives-up-youtube-chase/>

- Gavois, S. (2015) YouTube Red : tout ce qu'il faut savoir de l'offre sans publicité. *Nextinpact*. [Online]. [Accessed 11 October 2017]. Available from: <http://www.nextinpact.com/NEWS/97095-YOUTUBE-RED-TOUT-CE-QUIL-FAUT-SAVOIR-OFFRE-SANS-PUBLICITE.HTM>

- Gillmor, D. (2003) Google Buys Pyra: Blogging Goes Big-Time. Informatica. [Online]. [Accessed 11 October 2017]. Available from: <http://www.informatica.co.cr/internet/research/2003/0215.htm>

- Graham, J. (2005) Video websites pop up, invite postings. *USA Today*. [Online]. [Accessed 11 October 2017]. Available from: <http://usatoday30.usatoday.com/tech/news/techinnovations/2005-11-21-video-websites_x.htm>

- Grenier, F. (2007) YouTube prépare son lancement en France et en Europe. *Le Journal du Net*. [Online]. [Accessed 11 October 2017]. Available from: <http://www.journaldunet.com/ebusiness/internet/actualite/0706/070613-youtube-se-lance-en-france-et-en-europe.shtml>

- Gresh, K. (2007) The YouTube Guy (streaming). *IUP Magazine*. [Online]. [Accessed 11 October 2017]. Available from: <http://www.iup.edu/UPPER.ASPX?ID=51139>

- Hamedy, S. and Franklin, M. (2015) From Small Screens To Bookshelves. *Mashable*. [Online]. [Accessed 11 October 2017]. Available from: <http://mashable.com/2015/11/12/youtube-books-stream-con/#NvacQKnQqkqk>

- Hau, L. and Rosmarin, R. (2006) Why Buy YouTube? Why Not? *Forbes*. [Online]. [Accessed 11 October 2017]. Available from: <http://www.forbes.com/2006/10/06/youtube-google-video-tech-media-cx_lh_rr_1006google.html>

- Hoffman, J. (2009) Justin Bieber Is Living The Dream. *The New York Times*. [Online]. [Accessed 11 October 2017]. Available from: <http://www.nytimes.com/2010/01/03/fashion/03bieber.html?_r=0>

- Homonoff, H. (2015) YouTube Goes 'Over the Top'; Who Will Follow? *Forbes*. [Online]. [Accessed 11 October 2017]. Available from: <http://www.forbes.com/sites/howardhomonoff/2015/10/27/youtube-goes-over-the-top-who-will-fol-low/#55b8b5487b67>

- Hopkins, J. (2006) Surprise! There's a third YouTube co-founder. *USA Today*. [Online]. [Accessed 11 October 2017]. Available from: <http://usatoday30.usatoday.com/tech/news/2006-10-11-youtube-karim_x.htm>

- (2014) Justin Bieber. *Forbes*. [Online]. [Accessed 11 October 2017]. Available from: <http://www.forbes.com/profile/justin-bieber/>

- Kosoff, M. (2015) This is the first YouTube video ever uploaded — it was posted 10 years ago today. *Business Insider UK*. [Online]. [Accessed 11 October 2017]. Available from: <http://uk.businessinsider.com/first-youtube-video-2015-4?r=US&IR=T>

- Krazit, T. (2006) Google officialise le rachat de YouTube. *ZDNet*. [Online]. [Accessed 11 October 2017]. Available from: <http://www.zdnet.fr/actualites/google-officialise-le-rachat-de-you-tube-39363922.htm>

- La Monica, P. R. (2006) Google to buy YouTube for $1.65 billion. *CNN Money*. [Online]. [Accessed 11 October 2017]. Available from: <http://money.cnn.com/2006/10/09/technology/googleyou-tube_deal/index.htm?cnn=yes>

- Lawson, R. (2015) Did YouTube Just Ruin YouTube? *Vanity Fair*. [Online]. [Accessed 11 October 2017]. Available from: <http://www.vanityfair.com/culture/2015/10/youtube-digest-october-23>

- Madelaine, N. (2015) Apple Music a déjà dépassé Deezer avec 6,5 millions d'abonnés payants. *Les Échos*. [Online]. [Accessed 11 October 2017]. Available from: <http://www.lesechos.fr/tech-medias/hightech/021417632979-apple-music-a-deja-depasse-deezer-1167351.php>

- Marin, J. (2015) Face à Spotify et Apple Music, Youtube lance une offre musicale. *Le Monde*. [Online]. [Accessed 11 October 2017]. Available from: <http://siliconvalley.blog.lemonde.

fr/2015/11/13/face-a-spotify-et-apple-music-you-tube-lance-une-offre-musicale/>

- Moscaritolo, A. (2013) YouTube Founders Launch New Video-Sharing App MixBit. *PC Mag.* [Online]. [Accessed 11 October 2017]. Available from: <http://www.pcmag.com/article2/0,2817,2422849,00.asp>

- (No date) Most consecutive daily personal video blogs posted on YouTube. *Guinness World Records.* [Online]. [Accessed 11 October 2017]. Available from: <http://www.guinnessworldrecords.com/world-records/most-consecutive-daily-personal-video-blogs-posted-on-youtube/>

- O'Neill, M. (2010) 5 Ways YouTube Has Changed The World Forever. *Adweek.* [Online]. [Accessed 11 October 2017]. Available from: <http://www.ad-week.com/digital/youtube-changed-the-world/>

- Pillou, J. (2015) HTML – Langage. *Comment ça marche.* [Online]. [Accessed 11 October 2017]. Available from: <http://www.commentcamarche.net/contents/498-html-langage>

- Rauline, N. (2015) YouTube débarque à son tour sur le marché de la musique. *Les Échos.* [Online]. [Accessed 11 October 2017]. Available from: <http://www.lesechos.fr/tech-medias/medias/021473263765-youtube-debarque-a-son-tour-sur-le-marche-de-la-musique-1174617.php>

- Rees, M. (2008) Viacom autorisée à éplucher les logs des vidéos de YouTube. *Nextinpact.* [Online].

[Accessed 11 October 2017]. Available from: <http://www.nextinpact.com/archive/44607-viacom-google-youtube-mtv-logs.htm>

- Richaud, N. and Madelaine, N. (2015) YouTube sur les pas de Netflix. *Les Échos*. [Online]. [Accessed 11 October 2017]. Available from: <http://www.lesechos.fr/journal20151204/lec2_high_tech_et_medias/021530652870-youtube-sur-les-pas-de-netflix-1181495.php>

- Setra. (2015) YouTube Red, le nouvel abonnement qui devrait inquiéter Netflix et Spotify. *Presse Citron*. [Online]. [Accessed 11 October 2017]. Available from: <http://www.presse-citron.net/youtube-red-le-nouvel-abonnement-qui-devrait-inquieter-netflix-et-spotify/>

- Stelter, B. (2008) Some Media Companies Choose to Profit From Pirated YouTube Clips. *The New York Times*. [Online]. [Accessed 11 October 2017]. Available from: <http://www.nytimes.com/2008/08/16/technology/16tube.html>

- Stelter, B. (2008) YouTube Videos Pull In Real Money. *The New York Times*. [Online]. [Accessed 11 October 2017]. Available from: <http://www.nytimes.com/2008/12/11/business/media/11youtube.html?_r=0>

- (2007) Viacom International, Inc. v YouTube, Inc., No. 07 Civ. 2103: Text of complaint. *Viacom*. [Online]. [Accessed 11 October 2017]. Available from: <https://online.wsj.com/public/resources/

documents/ViacomYouTubeComplaint3-12-07.
pdf>

- Wakabayashi, D. (2015) Apple CEO Tim Cook:
  Apple Music Has 15 Million Users. *The Wall Street
  Journal*. [Online]. [Accessed 11 October 2017].
  Available from: <http://www.wsj.com/articles/
  apple-ceo-tim-cook-apple-music-has-15-million-
  users-1445319068>

- Woitier, C. (2013) Les internautes français
  préfèrent écouter de la musique sur YouTube.
  Le Figaro. [Online]. [Accessed 11 October 2017].
  Available from: <http://www.lefigaro.fr/secteur/
  high-tech/2013/09/25/32001-20130925ART-
  FIG00071-les-internautes-francais-preferent-ecou-
  ter-de-la-musique-sur-youtube.php>

- (2015) YouTube : dix ans d'existence et des vidéos
  devenues mythiques. *Sud Ouest*. [Online].
  [Accessed 11 October 2017]. Available from:
  <http://www.sudouest.fr/2015/02/14/youtube-
  dix-ans-d-existence-et-des-videos-devenues-
  mythiques-1830767-4803.php>

- (2015) Youtube fête ses 10 ans. *L'Express*. [Online].
  [Accessed 11 October 2017]. Available from:
  <http://lexpansion.lexpress.fr/high-tech/
  videos-les-10-ans-de-youtube-en-10-videos-me-
  morables_1651648.html>

ADDITIONAL SOURCES

- Google online support (Content ID): <https://support.google.com/youtube/topic/2778544?hl=en-GB&ref_topic=2676339>

- Google online support (Partner Programme): <https://support.google.com/youtube/answer/72851?hl=en-GB>

- Google press releases: <https://www.blog.google/press/>

- Guidiri, M. (2015) *Freemium*. Trans. Probert, C. Brussels: Plurilingua Publishing.

- YouTube press releases: <https://youtube.google-blog.com/>

- YouTube statistics: <https://www.youtube.com/intl/en-GB/yt/about/press/>

50MINUTES.com

IMPROVE YOUR GENERAL KNOWLEDGE
IN A BLINK OF AN EYE !

www.50minutes.com

www.50minutes.com

Ebook EAN: 9782808002400

Paperback EAN: 9782808002417

Legal Deposit: D/2017/12603/641

Cover: © Primento

Digital conception by Primento, the digital partner of publishers.